D0463906

God's Heart to a Man's Heart

God's Promises for Men of Faith

Tim Wesemann

www.timwesemann.com

~ In memory of David Moellenhoff, a
man of God, who knew the heart
of his heavenly Father and openly shared it
with his wife and children, family,
friends, co-workers, and all with whom
he came in contact.

www.ctainc.com

ISBN- 0-9718985-6-1

Unless otherwise indicated, all Scripture quotations are taken from the Holy Bible, King James Version
Copyright © 2003 by Christian Teachers Aid, 1625 Larkin Williams Rd., Fenton, MO 63026-2404.

Printed in Thailand

God's Heart to a Man's Heart
God's Promises for Men of Faith

Men
of
God

God knows you wrestle daily with complex and hurtful issues. He wants to get right into the midst of them with you. Will you let him? Will you reveal your heart (which he already knows ... you only think you're hiding it) and, in turn, take a good look at his heart?

You're right, men don't always put matters of the heart at the top of their "Favorite Things to Do" list. But that may change for you once you get a glimpse into the heart of your God and see there what he believes about you!

These poems (notes from God the Father to his sons—each of us) grew out of the letters God wrote to us in Holy Scripture. After you've read them, I urge you to go deeper by reading the Scripture passages at the top of each poem.

I pray you will hear Jesus' voice speaking his words of concern, compassion, and joy directly to your heart as you read and meditate on the words on these pages!

I pray that, more and more, you will see, in all of Scripture, God speaking his words directly to your heart. May the Holy Spirit work through this book, bringing out HIS best in you . . . from God's heart to your heart to the hearts of others.

Tim

For it pleased the Father that in
him should all fullness dwell; And,
having made peace through the
blood of his cross, by him to recon-
cile all things unto himself; by him,
I say, whether they be things in
earth, or things in heaven.

Colossians 1:19-20

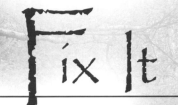

Fix It

Psalm 5:1-3; Psalm 22; Luke 18:27;
Colossians 2:13-15; Hebrews 12:2-3

"Fix it! Fix it!!" the cry goes up.
You love to hear those words, don't you,
my son?

But here's the problem:
        You run to your workroom
        and grab your tools.

I have the tools—the only tools—
        for repairing lives and hearts:
Two pieces of wood
        and three nails.

My tools are always available in
        my workroom,
located on the hill,
        at the intersection of
        Grace and Forgiveness.

P.S. By the way, I'll never say,
        "Fix it yourself!"

Fear thou not...Let not thine hands be slack. The Lord thy God in the midst of thee is mighty; he will save, he will rejoice over you with joy; he will rest in his love, he will joy over thee with singing.

Zephaniah 3:16-17

Quiet Time

Proverbs 11:2; Psalm 25:3; Zephaniah 3:17

Check your pride at the door, my son.
No room for embarrassment here either.

Leave all your shame
        hanging on that crossbeam
        with your guilt and sins.

You're not too old, too big, or too manly to
        climb into my lap.
        let me hold you and
        sing heaven's lullaby.

Rest.
Be refreshed.

Rest, be refreshed as I quiet you with my love
        and rejoice over you with singing.

[Jesus said,] "If I then, your Lord and Master,
have washed your feet; ye also ought to wash one
another's feet. For I have given you an example,
that ye should do as I have done to you."

John 13:14-15

Nice Serve

John 13:1-17

A basin.
Water.
A towel.
Your hands.
My heart.

The ball is in our court, my son
Good hand-heart coordination!
You balance joy and compassion well!
A soft touch.
Good focus!
Ahhh! Nice serve, dear servant . . .
very nice serve!
We make a good team!

. . . for the joy of the LORD is your strength.

Nehemiah 8:10

Plateful

1 Samuel 22.1-7; Psalm 33:20; 36:8; 55:1-5;
Isaiah 25:6; John 14:27; Romans 3:22-26; 15:13

You seem overwhelmed, my son.
I realize you have a lot on your plate.

I'm placing even more on that plate—
spiritually nourishing items,
that you'll relish.

Here's a large portion of my **peas**
        (It's not like the **peas** the world
has to offer.)

Live assured I will **meat** you where you are,
so **steak** your claim on my promises of hope
and help, and have an amazing **graze** on my
goodness!

Sit down next to me and feast!
For I am your Father.
I feed the nations.

P.S. Why don't people think I have a sense of
        humor?

Be ye angry, and sin not: let not the sun go down
upon your wrath: Neither give place to the devil.

Ephesians 4:26-27

Instead

John 14:2; Philippians 4:7; 1 John 1:7

Your anger screams so loudly
that at times you suspect
it shakes heaven's very foundation.
Impossible! My floors of grace stand firm!

You think it shakes your relationship with me,
but believe me, it never shakes my relationship
with you.

But your anger puts you on shaky ground with
those in your world:
family, friends, and co-workers.

Instead of losing your temper, stop . . .
        lose yourself in me.

Instead of pounding your feet on the floor,
        allow me to floor you with my grace.

Instead of raising your blood pressure,
allow my Spirit to raise your hands
        in praise to my Son
whose blood covers you with forgiveness,

He establishes my peace
in your heart,
in your life,
in your relationships.

I am crucified with Christ: nevertheless I
live; yet not I, but Christ liveth in me: and
the life which I now live in the flesh I live
by the faith of the Son of God, who loved
me, and gave himself for me.

Galatians 2:20

Running on Empty

Matthew 23:25-28; Galatians 2:17-21

You're the man—my man!
So let's talk—manly talk.
Like, what's under the hood?

350 engine. 5.0 liter V-8. Turbo booster, fuel-
injected, and plenty of horses!

Impressive!
But what's the real under-the-hood story, my son?
Let me run the engine diagnostics.

You're running on empty again, right?
Guilt-injected?
Ego-boosted?
Out of alignment with my will?

Check out my gift to you—Jesus Christ.
He's grace-injected,
Calvary-powered,
"V-won,"
a heart that runs on grace, and
a will perfectly aligned with my own.

The rest of your life is about to begin.
Do you hear my call?
Gentlemen, start your engines!
On his nailed-scarred marks, get set . . . GO!

*But now thus saith the LORD. . . Fear not: for I
have redeemed thee, I have called thee by thy
name; thou art mine. When thou passest
through the waters, I will be with thee; and
through the rivers, they shall not overflow thee.*

Isaiah 43:1-2a

Don't Be Afraid!

Psalm 139:13-16; Isaiah 43:1-3a

I formed you in your mother's womb.
I saw you when no one else could.
Yet you worry that I will fail you, my son.

Don't be afraid.
I still see you and love you just as I did back then.

You warily test life's waters with your toes.
But you can walk with confidence
            anywhere I lead you.

Yes, the current is swift,
but, remember, I am strong!
You doubt you can keep your balance on
the slippery rocks underfoot,
but, remember — I am your foundation.

Keep your eyes ahead, on the eddy's haven;
I'll keep you balanced and safe;
I am the Lord, your God, your Savior.

I formed you in your mother's womb.
I saw you when no one else could.
Don't be afraid.

For I know the thoughts that I think toward you, saith the LORD, thoughts of peace, and not of evil, to give you an expected end.

Jeremiah 29:11

Planning Sessions

Proverbs 15:22; Ecclesiastes 1:1-2; 2:1-11; Jeremiah 29:11;
John 3:16; Ephesians 1:3-8

You have plans for the day, don't you, my son?
I also have plans for you—
> Plans for your life.

You have dreams and hopes.
Let me shape your dreams and be your hope.

You plan for success, health, and happiness.
I give true prosperity, eternal health, abundant joy—
> all wrapped in my grace toward you
> in Jesus.

You have anchored your plans in the sands of
> human thoughts, dreams, wishes.
> I set my plans for you in
> the concrete of my covenant, on
> the bedrock of my eternal love.
I set my plans for you
> before the world's foundation.

Don't dream little human dreams.
Let me lead you.
Trust the plans I have for you.
I will make my dreams for you come true.

Blessed be the God and Father of our Lord
Jesus Christ, who hath blessed us with all
spiritual blessings in heavenly places in
Christ: In whom we have
redemption
through his
blood, the
forgiveness
of sins,
according to
the riches of
his grace ...

Ephesians 1:3, 7

What a Mess!

Job 3:26; Psalm 51; Romans 6:23; 7:15-25;
2 Corinthians 5:21; Colossians 1:19-20;
Hebrews 9:26-28

My son, what a mess you've made!
Entangled in sin. Handcuffed by guilt.
Poised perilously over a pit of failure

But you're not the only one.
My Son, on the cross, what a bloody mess!

Your sins entangled him on that cross.
There he took up your infirmities,
Here, now, he gifts you with forgiveness.

Handcuffed by nails,
pierced for your transgressions,
he once hung poised over the pit of hell's fire.
All to give you heaven.

Peace comes through his bloodied body,
            and forgiveness,
            and healing.

Good news for your messed up life!

God is our refuge and strength,
a very present help in trouble.
Therefore will not we fear,
though the earth be removed,
and though the mountains be carried into the midst
of the sea;
Though the waters thereof roar
and be troubled, though the mountains shake with
the swelling thereof.

Psalm 46:1-3

Creative Reflection

Proverbs 15:22; Psalm 46; 73:26; 77:11-15

My son, I appreciated your meditation on my word today.

You reflected on my power in terms of:
. . . the force of football linemen;
. . . the bulging arms of a homerun hitter;
. . . an awe-inspiring skyscraper;
. . . the majesty of the Grand Canyon.

The reflection was creative, but please remember:
. . . people fail to carry out plans;
. . . limbs break on people as well as trees;
. . . buildings crumble and fall;
. . . and I can fill in canyons by speaking
        a mere word.

I am your immovable line of defense.
My power knows no limits.
My might extends beyond all heights, all depths.

And I am your Father in Jesus, your Brother;
I love you more
than is humanly possible.

My soul melteth for heaviness: strengthen thou me according unto thy word.

Psalm 119:28

†

Cry for Strength

Exodus 15:2; 1 Chronicles 16:11; Psalm 63:1; John
20:19-21; 1 Timothy 1:2

My son, you are worn out.
Stop. Listen. And allow my Spirit to work.

You've packed your calendar so tight
you've sprung a leak
in your motivation.

I did not create you for chaos,
for such concentrated,
endless striving.

You cry out to me, "Strength!"
I answer, "Grace!"
Your prayer re-echoes through heaven's hallway,
"Please, give me strength!"

But listen ... listen to my voice, my promise:
"Instead of giving you strength,
I am going to be your strength!"

Rest in that.
Move forward in it—
Fortified.
Refreshed.

Wherefore seeing we also are compassed about with so great a cloud of witnesses, let us lay aside every weight, and the sin which doth so easily beset us, and let us run with patience the race that is set before us, looking unto Jesus the author and finisher of our faith; who for the joy that was set before him endured the cross, despising the shame, and is set down at the right hand of the throne of God. For consider him that endured such contradiction of sinners against himself, lest ye be wearied and faint in your minds.

Hebrews 12:1-3

Rely on Me

Joshua 1:5; Hebrews 12:1-3

If you insist on looking over your shoulder,
   gaze on the witnesses of my grace who
   surround you.

I told Joshua to do that as he journeyed to
the Promised Land:
"As I was with Moses, so I will be with you;
I will never leave you nor forsake you."

Leading a nation, a business, a household?
Here's my free(ing) advice:

   - Remember how I sustained others.
   - Rely on me.

Witnesses of my grace surround you!
Trust my presence and
the promises that envelop you.

Traveling mercies!
I will ever be your heavenly Father and partner
for the journey.

[Jesus said,] "Come unto me, all ye that labour and are heavy laden, and I will give you rest. Take my yoke upon you, and learn of me; for I am meek and lowly in heart: and ye shall find rest unto your souls. For my yoke is easy, and my burden is light."

Matthew 11:28-30

I'll? try an Apostrophe

Matthew 4:19; 10:32; 11:28; 28:20b; Luke 24:1-7;
John 6:40; 14:3; 15:4; Revelation 21:6

You can wallow there in self-pity
and make yourself *ill* or you can let your Brother
Jesus change those *Ills* forever—with only an
apostrophe.

He says to you:
I'll take your need for fulfillment, and
      I'll make you a fisher of men.
I'll take your angst in being unknown,
      and acknowledge you
      before my Father in heaven.
I'll take your burdens, and
      I'll give you rest.
I'll take your thirst for life, and
      I'll give you a drink from
      the spring of the water of life.
I'll take your fear of death, and
      I'll rise from the dead,
      while raising to life all
      who place their life in my hands.
I'll take your distress about being alone, and
      I'll send you the Holy Spirit to guide
      you into all truth.
Always remember, no matter what,
I'll be with you and remain in you-forever!

We are troubled on every side, yet not distressed; we are perplexed, but not in despair; persecuted, but not forsaken; cast down but not destroyed . . . For which cause we faint not, but though our outward man perish, yet the inward man is renewed day by day.

2 Corinthians 4:8-9, 16

Cross Words

2 Corinthians 4:1, 8-9, 16-18

My son, you don't have the strength to hold back
the walls now closing in on you.

Don't try!

Instead, stand at my Son's cross
while I use it to prop up
the walls of your life.

The cross beam won't collapse as
the walls close in on you.
The ceiling and floor of the world can't crush
the wood that held my Son.

My Son's cross will save you.
His perfect life will cover you.
The walls won't crush you!

Don't give up!
There is hope!
I've sent your rescuer!

*And Jesus said unto them, I am the bread of life: he that
cometh to me shall never hunger; and he that believeth on me
shall never thirst.*

John 6:35

Titled

Matthew 12:40; John 6:1-4, 35-40, 47-51;
Ephesians 5:23; Colossians 1:15-20

Your titles are some titles!
>> Bread Winner.
>> Head of the House.
Those titles come with a lot of pressure.

But listen to this truth:
Jesus Christ, is the real bread winner.
In fact, he is truly the Bread of Life;
No one who comes to him will hunger.

He's true man—a man like no other.
>> Perfect man.
>> One with me, the Father.

He's head of the body of believers,
>> My church.
>> My family.

Jesus is the Man; Bread Winner; the Head.

The pressure's off,
>> since Jesus was on
—on the cross for you!

I just wanted you to know.

Incline your ear, and come unto me: hear, and your soul shall live; and I will make an everlasting covenant with you, even the sure mercies of David.

Isaiah 55:3

Sensing Salvation ~ Hearing

1 Samuel 3:11; 2 Samuel 7:22-24; 1 Kings 19:11-13; Proverbs 20:12; Isaiah 55:3; Matthew 13:16-17

My son, as I've watched over you,
I've noticed your senses
always on alert.
And yet, you miss so much.

Noise bombards your ears;
you tune out a good portion—
of necessity, of course.

Still, I regret that
You often miss a world of words—my words:
heaven-directed,
heaven-sent songs;
sounds of encouragement—even
in the silence.

Be selective, my child, but take care to
Tune in to my words of
Wisdom, Love, and Guidance.
Listen to my voice
reverberating through history:

I love you!
I love you!
I love you!

Now thanks be unto God, which always causeth us to tri-umph in Christ, and maketh manifest the savour of his knowledge by us in every place. For we are unto God a sweet savour of Christ, in them that are saved . . .

2 Corinthians 2:14-15

Sensing Salvation~ Smell

Hosea 14:1-2, 4-6; 2 Corinthians 2:14-15; Philippians 3:19-20

Some scents pique your interest, my son;
> but you need to ignore them:
> the fragrant temptation to self-indulgence,
> the lust-evoking perfume of a passing woman,
> the enticing aroma of hurtful foods.

Rather, allow scents of salvation to capture your attention:
> the sweet bouquet of my grace,
> the gift of my life-breathing Spirit,
> the warm aroma of Bread that never spoils.

I allow 180-degree turns.
> In fact, I encourage them!
> My Spirit knows your needs.
> Rely on his perfect sense when tempted.
> He will guide you toward
>> the sweet essence of my grace.

So Jesus had compassion on them, and touched
their eyes: and immediately their eyes received
sight, and they followed him.

Matthew 20:34

Sensing Salvation ~ Touch

Matthew 9:20-21; 20:34; Mark 1:41; Luke 24:39

A woman once touched
the hem of my Son's garment
          and found healing.

You touch others so generously,
          and receive their touch
          selflessly.
I've noticed!

My fingerprints cover your days.
          These are no partial prints.
Instead, your life evidences
          full and clearly defined touches of
          my eternal grace,
          my unchanging Word,
          my loving discipline.

My touch has left an impression.
It has changed you forever.

That pleases me.

*O taste and see that the LORD is good: blessed is the
man that trusteth in him. O fear the LORD, ye his saints:
for there is no want to them that fear him . The young
lions do lack and suffer hunger: but they that seek the
LORD shall not want any good thing.*

Psalm 34:8-10

Sensing Salvation ~ Taste

Psalm 34:8-10; Ezekiel 3:3; 1 Peter 2:2-3

I love being the Giver
of heavenly flavors.

I want you to learn the art
of the connoisseur!

Like Ezekiel, learn to appreciate
my Word—
sweet as honey.

Take and drink, my pure,
life-giving milk:
my kindness in Christ!

You will grow strong in faith
as you feast on my food,
having tasted that I am good.

My son, attend to my words;
incline thine ear unto my sayings.
Let them not depart from thine eyes;
keep them in the midst of thine heart.
Let thine eyes look right on,
and let thine eyelids look straight before thee.
Ponder the path of thy feet,
and let all thy ways be established.
Turn not to the right hand nor to the left:
remove thy foot from evil.

Proverbs 4:20-21, 25-27

Sensing Salvation — Sight

Psalm 46:8-11; Proverbs 4:20-27; Isaiah 58:7-9a; Matthew 13:16-17;
John 19:25-27; 1 Corinthians 13:12; Hebrews 2:8-9; 12:2

Son, do you see what I see?
I realize your sight is limited.
But there's so much I want you to see –
gifts I daily place in front of you:

The hurting who need my compassion;
The thirsty who need a drink of living water;
The lonely who long for a lone friend;

I see a cross
where the world needs to come
for forgiveness.

Join me there now
Bring your friends.
I am about to do a great thing!
The blind will see and respond,
"Surely this is the Son of God!"
Heaven's gates will be opened!
A new vision, given to my people.

Do you see?
Forgiveness! Grace! Life! Hope!

It's all yours . . .
from your Father!

And the Word was made flesh, and dwelt among us,
(and we beheld his glory, the glory as of the only
begotten of the Father,) full of grace and truth.
And of his fulness have all we received, and grace
for grace.

John 1:14, 16

Sensing Salvation

Romans 11:36

Taste and see!
        I, your Lord, am good!

At the cross of Jesus you'll see the truth . . .
up close and personal.

Taste tears of joy
        at his empty tomb,
        now brimming with life.

Cry out—by day, by night:
        "Touch me, Savior, and I will live!"

You will live!

Be prepared
        for my life-changing touch.

Breathe in
        the scent of grace and new life
        through my Spirit.

Hear this, my child, whom I love:
Your sins are forgiven.
        Your senses are set free.
        Free to serve me, as you serve others.

Touch, taste, smell, hear and see that I am,
        and will always remain,

Your good and gracious Lord and Savior.